A Pagan Bramble Patch

A Pagan Bramble Patch

Poems

By Stephen Dohrmann

Zion Publishing

Copyright © 2018 Stephen Dohrmann

All rights reserved. No part of this product may be reproduced in any manner whatsoever without written permission, except in the case of brief quotations embodied in critical articles and reviews.

Cover graphic created by author from a photo by Vivian L. Lee

Back cover photo by Vivian L. Lee

ISBN: 978-0-9998819-5-8

Available online.

For bulk order information contact the author at:

dohrmannstephen@gmail.com

Zion Publishing
Des Moines, Iowa
www.zionpublishing.org

To Vivian

Contents

Prologue – The Awen-Coin	2
The Leap	4
Looking for the Next to Last Book of Poems	5
After Amergin	7
Locking Eyes with the Bear	9
Footprints and Myths	10
Wilder Nature	12
Born on the Day the Bard Was Born	14
Bramble Patch	15
Equinox	16
Stacking Wood	17
Bearing the Weight	18
Eating a Meal Well	19
First Samhain	20
Samhain Villanelle	22
Ancestors	23
Autumn Scolds	25
Homespun Fire	26
The Lake Is Frozen Over	27
Supplicant	28
Shanty Down	29
Spirit Song of the Red Lynx	30
Winter Solstice	31
The Darktime Cord Has Slipped Its Knot	33
After Imbolc	34
Vernal Equinox	35
Ostara	37
Spring Rite	38
A Way of Digging	39
When All our Words Have Been Turned	41

Canticle for Beltane	42
A Brief Epithalamion	43
Tricklestream	44
Dandelion Credo	45
Midsummer at Terrapin Branch	46
Trout Fishing	48
The God Is a Black Bear	49
Late Ghost	50
A Quiet in the Weather	51
The Fawn	52
Dryspell	54
Cooler Nights	56
Hickory Grain	58
The Rattlesnake	59
Moving from the Country to the Town	61
Elemental Blessing	63
On a Windy Day in a New Place	64
Boundary Stones	65
If I Have Found My Way Here	67
Bendithia Ni Braid	68
Looking Back	70
Let Us Let Go	71
Transmigrations	72
Be as Air	73
All Things Are Full of Gods	74
Now in the Urbs, We Meet New Gods	76
To Greet the Gods	77
New Pagan Gods Are Dancing	78
Spirits and Sprites	79
Bast	80
Strange Poems	81
Tuatha Dé Danann	82

Janus	84
A Hole in the World	86
Staring Hard at the Chessboard	87
Whimsy	89
Two Minds	90
Beware the Single-Faced Person	91
Far from those Celtic Shores	92
Go Down Dying	93
Singing of Sun and Fire	94
Tabula Rasa	95
Mae	96
Then There Is the Waiting	100
Brigid in the City	101
Isles of the Blest	102
Unpacking for the Journey	103
The Word-Bag	105
A Man with Seven Sticks	107
Cage of Swords	108
Magister Fortunae	109
Butterfly Effects	110
Wherever All the Rivers Run	112
Belief	113
As the Moon Waxes	114
Epilogue – Becoming the Sun	115
Acknowledgments	117

And I fall asleep with the gods, the gods
that are not, or that are
according to the soul's desire,
like a pool into which we plunge, or do not plunge.

—D.H. Lawrence, "There Are No Gods"

A Pagan Bramble Patch

Prologue – The Awen-Coin

Brigid, though you reign over
fresh water and hearth,
you are no domestic deity
tamed to town or temple nave,

but goddess of the red-gold sun,
amber blaze in the honeycomb,
raging of the red-fire forge,
warrior of the rowan-spear—

and patron of the poet's craft
with its many-tongued flames.

Brigid, lend to me at least a small
awen-coin, etched with sparks,
to strike against the cold torchstone—

to kindle fire from a bundle,
cradled in the imaginal forge,
of spell-braided talisman-runes

and images rough-hewn in the soul
from before we belabored the soil:

figures painted in ancient caves
of hands, and gods of the hunt,
seeming to move in flickering light—

or simple lines, drawn out from dreams,
by a child with a stick in the sand—

The Awen-Coin ...

that I might conjure and shape,
from these visions and signs,
the lineaments of new song.

*Brigid of the sun-fire awen flame,
lend to me at least a small etched coin—*

Awen: spirit-flow, including poetic inspiration; perhaps even vibrating cosmic strings that weave the contours of our worlds.

The Leap

    Teetering between two realms,
                            dipping my toe
  into waters on both sides,
      I feel the alluring rush
    of deep-running rivers,
      pleasurable undercurrents
              that strive

to pull me in
    to deeper, drowning depths.

Yet to keep pure
   —from either common world or dream—
is its own kind of death:
              pristine deceit
      of ascetic denial,
        righteousness wrapped
  in thorns and stiff robes,
the unwrinkled mirror
    of an unmoving mind.

Entranced by the currents on both sides,
    I learn to survive

  —not by stillness, but by abandon—

to leap—
        attuned to the tides' untamed beat,
not by my thoughts
          —but the pulse in my feet.

Looking for the Next to Last Book of Poems

> "Nearly all my life I've noted that some of my thinking was atavistic, primitive, totemic. This can be disturbing to one fairly learned."
>
> —Jim Harrison, *Songs of Unreason*

Looking for the next to last book of poems
(stuck in the back of some hard-packed shelf)
by that rumbling American renegade,
Jim Harrison—whose voice was rough-rubbed stone,
smoldering thunder, a growl from the belly
of a one-eyed bear, whose living eye burned
like the sun in a chestnut—it came to me
that every poem should be a totem.

We should cast our words like fire-throated runes
—even if unadorned and plainly wrought—
with scorched intent and savage utterance,
intoxicated with drumbeat and sweat—
dancing, even gracelessly, till falling,
exhausted in the dust—as we still sing,
grasping for the last rasp of a whisper
to keep the fevered fetich-wheel spinning—

The poet should be a mad shaman-priest,
(city-dweller or druid in the wood)
scrying the cave of the soul for visions,
barely glowing in the dark—like long-lived
embers buried under ash—whose fire
might be breathed into a resurrection,
a glimmering enchantment to entice
the refugee gods to reveal themselves.

Looking for the Next ...

>Always the risk: the totem fails to leap
>to life, and the gods carry on, disguised
>in their everyday masks, passing by
>without a blessing, or a glance of grace.

After Amergin

> "The English poetic education should, really, begin not with the *Canterbury Tales*, not with the *Odyssey*, not even with *Genesis*, but with the *Song of Amergin*...."
>
> —Robert Graves, *The White Goddess: A Historical Grammar of Poetic Myth*

I am the hummingbird
who darts in the sun
I am the hawk
who hunts on high wind
I am the owl
who haunts the upland moor
I am the lynx
who prowls like a ghost
in the witch-twilight hours
I am the bear
whose growl echoes low
in the deep thicket wood

I am the eyes
that flash in the lightning
I am the fire
that burns in the stones
I am the drum
that beats in the root
I am the muse
who whispers in tongues
mystical messages
from inside the bark

After Amergin …

    I am a sign
    in the veins of a leaf
    I am a sigil
    that spins in the wind
    I am a song
    that sings in creekwater
    lyrical madrigals
    in a quick-hearted stream

    I have a name
    whose telling is secret
    I have a name
    that nobody knows
    whose murmur is the lure
    of a magickal spell
    in a song and a growl
    from woodland or fell—

Locking Eyes with the Bear

Once, as a boy, I unwittingly chased a black bear from a stand of weeds taller than I was. And, still not knowing what I had flushed out, I followed through the trampled path his big body made, into a stand of open woods.

There he turned and stood, slowly raising himself up the way that bears do, drawing up along his spine, to get a better look. Maybe thirty feet away. Standing tall.

Locking eyes with a small boy, now rooted on the spot. After what seemed like a longer time than it surely was, he lowered himself to all fours, casually turned away and ambled off, just as casually. Maybe he was thinking, "Stupid human boy."

And still I remember
locking eyes with the bear.

Footprints and Myths

I have too many ancestors, scattered
across a wide ancestral terrain.
Their genetic markers are like bright pins
stuck in the map of four continents,
with little but mingled blood in my veins—
and stories and dreams—to connect them.

There is a single marker to mark me
to this land: a soft footprint embedded
in the flesh of Turtle Island. The tales
told by First People of themselves begin
not in Asia—but with Sky Woman
or the Four Worlds. We should listen to them.

At root, it is myths tell us who we are—
our own myths, or those of our grandmothers.
Our grandmothers ought to be believed
without proof from documents or tests.
And dreams should not be hastily dismissed.
I choose to believe those varied voices.

I am a man of many peoples,
who have travelled many lands. To track them
would require the remainder of my years—
and still the trail would not become home.
I embrace them all, like sacred smoke:
let the smoke drift in the wind where it will.

I am a river of many streams,
mingled of memory, myth and dreams.

Footprints and Myths ...

Or I might descend from the Bear People.

They were the First Gods of many elder clans, far back in time. I have a Bear name in a northern language. A Bear sign guards the northern stars, protector of that domain.

Maybe my forebears came from there—

Wilder Nature

    (For my brother, Jeff)

We did not grow up in wilder nature,
though we grew up near: across the two creeks
there was a mountain, if a fingerling,
whose tip overlooked the Susquehanna

—the West Branch—and Great Island upriver,
a place of meeting for the Andaste
and Lenape long before farm-seeking
settlers imagined there was a land here.

That mountain had deer trails to skirt the bluffs,
and if you followed those trails far enough
you found the larger, rugged watershed
forest, restricted from human traffic.

Big Creek (we called it) was formed from higher
spring-fed streams running quick and cold through rough
ravines, where red-tailed hawks struck from high air,
the deer grew fat on acorns and berries

—not corn—and the brown trout were all native,
unbred. To hunt or fish you had to trek
in the way the deer did: small-footed paths
laid down and kept by the Four-Footed Tribes—

or along an abandoned logging road
and under some fences, now forgotten
by foresters of past years, we were sure.
We claimed passage based on more ancient right.

Wilder Nature ...

We hiked, hunted and fished there—and sometimes
came across the track of the black-bear god.
Never did we take more than fair limit
for table, according to hallowed law

from primal time, still honored in our creed.
So many days did we fare in those woods,
touching earth lightly so as not to leave
a footmark—nor mar the bountiful wild.

A little after darkfall we'd be home.
We lived, not in the wilderness—just near.

∾

My brother still lives there. I have moved on.
And his memory is likely better
than mine.
        Though I am of wilder nature,
the wildness in his nature is less tamed.

Born on the Day the Bard Was Born

Born on the day the Bard was born, and born
on the day he died (or so I have heard),
I am a man of more than my father's years—
and yet dreaming inside resides a child:

a child who played with pirates in the wood,
a fallen tree for a stout ship, a stick
to swing for a cutlass; lying in wait
in the briarthorns like a highwayman,
leaping out at a stagecoach made of wind;
wading across the creek, now river Styx;
defending our castle in the rock cliffs,
an abode called "The Coffins" for the shape
of stones—larger than a young lad—that lay
below the cliff walls, in what had become
the dungeon. (I could hear chains in that place,
for prisoners who had died at the hand
of some long-ago king—hoary voices
haunted twisty, phantastical hallways.)

I would play again with gusto among
those old ghosts of make-up and make-believe,
jousting in the theaters of my mind,
where day-by-day I lived and fought and died—
and always was born again. Now the child
hides in the man—and dreams again to be born.

Bramble Patch

My brain must resemble a bramble patch—
my thoughts so easily snagged on bright thorns
and torn from the intended path, gone lost
amid the tangles. "Who goes there?" I call
aloud to myself—only an echo
answers. I do not recognize the voice.

I have many imaginary friends,
and any one of them might be playing
tricks. "Who goes there?" What password can I hold
like a keepsake, touching to remember?
The terrain is always changing, and I
cannot keep up as the briars catch me.

Sometimes, from inside this barbed labyrinth,
the sun seems to surround everywhere,
offering neither direction nor time
of day to reckon by. I stagger on
without divining a destination,
scrambling through the bramble patch of my brain.

Equinox

The hummingbirds have departed, leaving
their absence behind, like a small dying
into shrinking days and darkening months.

Hope is remembering how the seasons
return and return in their weathered round,

how birds no bigger than a baby's fist
will travel twice a thousand miles along
a wind-held rosary, from equinox
to equinox, bearing in their quick hearts
remembrance—of a small resurrection
into longer-lived days and summer light.

Stacking Wood

For days an iron-cast sky
has weighed heavily on the valley,
like the lid on a stockpot
whose leftover stew has grown cold—

Stacking wood, I remember
how, for the first time in years,
my friend of many seasons
will not join me
by the winter fires.

Bearing the Weight

The axe and maul are heavier,
and splitting a harder chore—
but winter will hardly wait.

Muscle-ache, and stinging sweat
pouring from open pores,
mock me for my aging state.

Chilling air keeps me at my task
as gray light grows darker,
till I am cloaked in slate—

reminded as I limp away,
that I will never again
walk with an even gait.

That is the fate of years,
and not to be mourned—
just the way that I bear the weight.

Eating a Meal Well

Eating a meal well entails
some conviviality
even if just with yourself
and of course the present gods
who simply want to be seen
if even in the mind's eye

flickering playful figures
who only want you to laugh
if you happen to glimpse them
over meat and roasted corn
and flagons of dark red wine
by the embers of a fire

even an imagined fire
breathed into life long ago
by forgotten ancestors
who also saw the same gods
who visited ancient fires
who had voices but no names

who will visit us today
if only we welcome them
in conviviality
to the tables of our age—

First Samhain

> (For Andrea and Robert, wherever they may be)

A simple meal: lasagna,
greens and warm thick bread,
enough wine and convivial
conversation to soften a soul
that might have been brittled
by a wire-edged work-day—

Some brief rubrics explained
so each could participate
in the rite—script prearranged,
    though the setting
      was homely, good-humored,
    sweatshirts and jeans—
with a small Samhain fire
in the brownstone fireplace.

We all sat easy on the floor
till rendering our turns
in the turning of elements
around the sacred circle.
    (I learned how hard it can be
    to guide a hand-held flame
    through the west-water quarter,
    till given grant to go on.)

Another year gathered in,
the eve of winter-beginning—
    leaves fallen and falling
    in the wet night outside—

First Samhain ...

ancestors and spirits welcomed,
blessings offered and asked,
acquaintances becoming friends—
    ending the evening
    with cakes and dark apple ale—

"Merry meet, and merry part,
till merry meet again!"

Samhain is pronounced "Sowen."

Samhain Villanelle

Now is come the eve of the Samhain drum:
time betwixt the rippling years
with harvest in, a new season begun.

Quick match-fire touch to spark the festive flame,
gather in close, arm-in-arm—
for now is the eve of the Samhain drum.

The ancient spirits have not departed
nor ancestors gone away
with harvest in, a new season begun:

friends from near worlds, as well as this dear place,
plait their souls along with ours,
and join us this eve of the Samhain drum.

For never need anyone be alone,
no matter where we might dwell
with harvest in, a new season begun—

in dense city block or a hermit's den,
bright spirits invite themselves
when the eve is come for the Samhain drum,
with harvest in, a new season begun.

Ancestors

I can hear them singing. Their voices
sound like my own,
but the words are forgotten—
they got lost somewhere
in the narrow places:
tightening arterial alleyways
of insufferable judgment,
walls of great stones laid by hands
calloused by grief and guilt
until, under the final weighty stone
laid down, the edifice entire collapses,
driving an exodus in fearful disarray
out from the aching, encumbered Egypt
of my own inhabited past—

Not every tune from those times was tragic—
but under the capricious melody
of all my memories
—whether meandering walled-in streets,
or spacious courtyards inviting
music, lemon-blooms and light—
I can hear their voices singing.

And I long to join them—
but I am become a stranger,
time-burnt denizen of a no-man's-land
whose far-flung horizons
and dizzying, unhindered sky
had themselves been a beckoning
to unfettered dreams—and hope—
and whose cool oases offered respite
as well as escape: shade and shelter,
pomegranates, poetry and peace.

Ancestors ...

    The wilderness became a safer place
    than the civilized avenues,
    alleyways and streets I left behind.

    But even as a nomad, I could hear them
    singing on the other side,
    the far side of the river
    —river of radiance,
    river of shimmering light—
    in a language whose rhythms
    were like the calling of water
    to water, fire to fire,
    drumming to a once familiar heartbeat
    in a language whose words
    were lost to me,
    but whose calling I could hear.

    I can hear them now,
    just on the other side of light.
    I can hear the water.
    I can hear the fire.
    I can hear the pulsing drum.

    I can hear them singing.
    I can hear them singing—

Autumn Scolds

Autumn scolds me now
   with the rub of a rough hand
the wind
      scrapes inside my thin shirt

Maple leaves are tawny red
   like wild apples
         and the grass
has grown too long for winter

My neighbors all have finished
   the last of their mowing

Darkness moves in close enough
   to tug my ears
     songs
   from my blues harp
          stagger
      aimlessly
           down
    the hill
      a dog
is barking on a chain

and all my tools rust in the yard.

Homespun Fire

    Winter has visited early this year,
    with misty frost and frigid air—
        as the sun
          steals further south.

    But there is homespun warmth
        to be drawn
    from earth-stored sunfire—long laid away
          deep underground;
    in dormant roots; in bark; in brittle,
        seasoned kindling sticks,
      and husks;
    even in the sealed heart
              of antediluvian stones.

    Strike a flint to starburst stone
        or steel,
           catch a spark:
    the gathered kindling
              smolders,
        flares and flames.

    Slowly lay on
           the maple, ash and oak.
    As dried wood crackles,
        and the hearth heats up,
    swirls of smoke
            —hosts of ghosts—
      flee up the well-brushed flue.

    Even as winter
           weighs down with chill air,
      our homespun fire
        wraps around us
      a warm-quilted cheer.

The Lake Is Frozen Over

The lake is frozen over.
The geese are gone on their southern round,
the ground sleeps under wind-crusted snow.
I remain for the season.

I remain, though the geese have gone,
and others have gone—
and even in my remaining
I continue in the turning
of my threadbare time, year on year,

as the sky continues turning
on some long-forgotten hub,
turning the stars, season on season,
the cold untiring cosmic wheel.

Supplicant

    Sitting before an empty page—
    like a supplicant before an altar,
    waiting for the god or spirit
    to appear—a glass of spirits,
    fired with peat, keeps—in the late hour,
    narrowly awake—a naive faith alive,
    a eucharistic faith in words
    to transubstantiate heartbeat and breath
    into sound and magick and grace—

    even a very small grace—a comfort,
    a paltry song, a tale of far-away,
    a ragged caravan to carry our cares
    across the night-sky to another land—
    so that we might rest, if only
    for the smallest hour, in the charity
    of a gentle spirit or god—
    one who might come with warmth from the stove,
    or splash of light in a smoky window,
    or a feathery whisper on fine air—
    or even in the crisp, clean space
    of an ordinary, white-washed page—

    waiting for words to awaken
    the heartbeat and breath—into sound.

    I am a supplicant, biding the night
    in front of an empty altar
    for the god or spirit to appear,
    bearing even a paltry grace:

    a stammering tale of far-away—

Shanty Down

The year is nearly new in Shanty Down—
when the world will turn back toward the sun,
the calendar kept in the walnut grain
will mark another band behind the bark,
and all the wee folk will wake from their nap.

Spring is still a long way off—but the roots
will warm in their own time, and Shanty Down
will bask in season, all golden and green;
the wee folk will sharpen their springtime tools;
the bear-god will fish again in the creek,

as kingfisher scolds; the red lynx will prowl
deeper, and more ghost-like, in the thick wood;
and Shanty Down, though quiet now, will ring
with clatter, laughter and wild-hearted song.
Yet a few weeks, the small village must sleep—

but if you chance on Shanty Down come spring,
and listen clear—you'll hear the wee folk sing.

Spirit Song of the Red Lynx

I am the Red Lynx
whose heart is the wild—

a wraith untamed
haunting in dreamtime
shape-shifting flame
through deep-twilight wood

who hides in the light
as a shimmer of light
who moves with the wind
as a whisper of wind

who stalks the forest
soft-footed as air
who sees much further
than he can be seen

always alone
in the in-between
where suntime twines with night
or dark is laced with dawn

keeper of secrets
keeper of dreams—
I am the Red Lynx
whose heart is the wild

always alone
in the in-between.

Winter Solstice

Woodsmoke tells the snowy moon
of a heckling hickory fire
that keeps the hearthstone warm
    —this morning's chore to carry logs
    from the abandoned barn
    up to the cottage for burning—
as we regale ourselves with tales
from days of a taller sun,

when green men ran like shadows
in the oak-and-cedar grove,
fat trout flashed in bright pools,
cider-apples swelled with juice,
and sparrows argued,
greedy among the blackberry thorns—

days of grander stature
and swaggering light,
recollected this midwinter's eve
with bandied songs
and bawdy, made-up spells.

Tonight is the solstice
    —with a strong moon waxing as witness—
when winterberry holly boughs we lay
along the mantel beam,
and drink hot brandy braced
with nutmeg and cinnamon,
    —throwing spoonsful in the flames
    with wishes for the coming year—

Winter Solstice ...

    until the embers glow low on the grate,
    the dawn sifts like pale ash
    through the leaf-bare limbs,
    the great blue heron lifts his long body
    up from the darkwater creek
    as a bleak mist rises
    from the snowy ground,

    and the midwinter spirits feebly wake
    to whisper on shivering breath

        their age-old names.

The Darktime Cord Has Slipped Its Knot

The darktime cord has slipped its knot—the days
are lengthening again. And though the trees
still are bare of all but the crispest leaves,
there is promise promised in just the hours
that keep the light—and gather moments more
each day, like pages added to a book.

But I neither mind the winter, nor mourn
the night. Ricks of wood, split and stacked in fall,
extend the hours we need not hibernate.
Apples we harvested at summer's end
and dried, homebrewed wine bottled months ago,
novels we recall we've wanted to read—

and time to share ourselves: these keep us well
through shrinking days—and days that start to swell.

After Imbolc

The stubborn winter remains with us yet—
a swift-running wind, cold as a wolf's howl,
a cowl of heavy-woven snow conceals
the clear, undimmed but ice-encrusted eyes
of the god crouched low in the dark oak wood:
Cernunnos the antlered, scrying for light.

Brigid's mantle, flung from the sun's far fire
at Imbolc, has not settled round us yet,
though her other, earth-hold fire dances high
in the red hearth. No need to keep the cold
in bones till spring: Brigid's glad gleaming flame
will warm us—and her mantle melt the snow

in March, when the god of darkwood bows down
and Brigid of the Sun reclaims her crown.

Vernal Equinox

The moment of balance,
of seeming equipoise,
is only the illusion of a lull,
intermission in the breathing
between day and night,
or hesitation at the edge of

the turning of the hourglass,
the tipping of the scales,
the changing
of some seasonal guard.

Time never stops—nor runs
in a logical line
toward some future point called *Then*,
that afterward we might remember—
but spirals round-and-round
some god or strange attractor,
spinning itself into an Indra's Net
of never-ending fractals, flashing
from *Whenever.*

There is no still point
in the turning world.

We confuse ourselves
by the ticking of our clocks
—the pendulum's pause,
the space between the clicks—
and encode that confusion
in the tense of our thoughts.

Vernal Equinox ...

       ஐ

    The geese who are gone over winter
    return to the lake our porch overlooks.

Ostara

A sunhawk sways over the springlake
like the passing of a magician's hand,
flashing red flame on the water.
Maples are newly leaved with fire.
Yesterday I saw a bee, barely born,
staggering in the forsythia.
The grass is a green resurrection
rooted in the warm flesh of earth.

Ostara's dawn seeds the land with light.
Till midsummer solstice, the waxing days
claim their hours from the tithing of night.

Spring Rite

The goats knock heads, lock
thick alpine horns,
back off—arch way up
on strong hind legs

from which they launch
sinew-rippling bodies
into headlong attack—
each blow a rifle-crack

whose sharp echo
shatters the hour
of sunrise calm
in the slim-hipped valley—

battering each other
again and again,
till the smaller one
lies down—

and then his brother
lies down,
both of them panting
in dew-bent grass—

the contest, for now,
decided.

A Way of Digging

    The pickaxe breaks into chunks the clay soil,
a loosening-up for later planting—
a hand-blistering ritual of sweat,
cramped fingers, aching wrists and arms, a back
that will not easily unbend itself
after an hour of bowing to labor.
Breathing in muted grunts, I try to work
the word-sounds of prayer into the work, prayers
to the unnamed gods who live in this place
with us—and ages have.

                Falling darkness
will enshroud the day long before the task
is finished—and sleep will painfully come.
Tomorrow, I will turn the broken soil,
once again by hand, with invocations
and spade, mixing in some compost and sand
for drainage, and to ease the earthy path
of frail-fingered roots.

                Neighbors offered
the loan of a powerful, gas-driven
tiller that I could walk behind, sparing
my back that suffers from old injury,
while doing the job in far fewer hours.
They mistake the plainness of my purpose.
The garden is not my meaning, nor time
my coin—and the labor is more than means:
my body itself the prayer-wheel I turn
through my muscles and nerves, with ragged breath
catching my throat, bowing down, turning soil,
over and over, rolling round the wheel ....

A Way of Digging ...

∞

I have always been much less a farmer,
or even gardener, than a hunter:
stalking the game, light-footed in the leaves,
listening to move with the shifting wind,
measuring my time, and breathing that time
on the out-breath, making sure of the shot—

But now has become a time for turning
the soil—and a time that must be taken.

When All Our Words Have Been Turned

When all our words have been turned and turned,
like flowers tossed in a stormy breeze
till wind-burnt and bruised, bereft
of the brightness we once beheld in them
when first we set them out in the sun—

in a quiet hour, I consider
how the hummingbirds madly dart
among scarlet impatiens
without debate or invitation,
having borne themselves on many winds,
turned and turned, until turning
into this corner of our garden
to dance and mate the summer season,

mocking without intention
our laborious chains of reason.

Canticle for Beltane

    I have wandered without a calendar
        now a long time
    and no longer remember
        the canon of days

    But today I know is written
        in the Book of Waking
    This day brightly lit with the first flame
        of summerfire

    is a most high holy day
        broken open
    like bread leavened from light
        and bearing the aroma

    of warm wine pouring from new fruit
        in the strawberry beds
    whose blossoms were hosts in spring
        to choirs of humming bees

    And though the proper prayers
        have been forgotten
    Nature's own glossolalia sings
        a sensual psalm

    Let the liturgy begin!

A Brief Epithalamion

By sun-enlivened bees aroused
to quivering, full-veined passion,
a swollen bud must cleave its flesh
to consummate the season.

Tricklestream

    Smallstream
           crinkle-crackle
      over flatrock

                through riffle-stones
          mist-licked
            fleeced by moss
        where the skinny path

sneaks
        from brush-cedar
     briarthorn
          thicket
        into thistle-field

    tricklestream
        in tall grass
habitat
        for slither-snakes

   Shhh!

Dandelion Credo

If nothing else, I believe in Dandelions—
and ask of them no favors, except
a scattering of sunlight in the grass,
a wild fermenting in the root.

You too are invited to enroll
in this heretical, ribald religion:

summers delirious with yellow flowers,
autumns drunk with sunlit wine.

Midsummer at Terrapin Branch

Into midsummer tall days come, striding like kings
with green eyes, wearing plum-stained robes and
    golden crowns
gleaming high as the cathedral-spire sun at noon,
to our cottage on the creek called Terrapin Branch—

The kingfisher rattles his voice at the heron,
high priest of the creekwater, and clear light casts
crinkling-bright nets in the current and rocky pools,
where quicksilver fish scatter quicker than a blink

if you lean in too close. Summer bees are minstrels
thrumming among the new melons and cucumbers
in our sun-wheel garden; hummingbirds cavort
in crimson beebalm; towering sunflowers loom

over the warm brick walkways, laid out like ley lines
to travel the eight-wind rose rounding out the wheel.
Mornings shimmer like polished doubloons, afternoons
burn deeper, like rubies, as the sun rubs the west.

Heavy heat-thunder murmurs, crickets come alive,
fireflies flash their faery torches in falling gloom,
and soon the druid-owls will drone their mournful psalms
in the cedar-oak wood, with somber shadows hung

under a swelling moon. The night will be sultry
and short, as ghostly night-hunters hunt without blame
in high-ridge forest or thistled, creek-meadow field—
and echo their killing-cries down the winding glen.

Midsummer at Terrapin Branch ...

But soon the clinging gown of darktime falls away
as another tall day, with gold-glimmering crown
and green eyes, strides into tomorrow, innocent
of yesterday's doings under the sun or moon.

Trout Fishing

(For Scott)

Barbarian waters cascade
swift and deep over rocky crevasses
where the trout lie, feeding ruthlessly—

The filament silently slices the air,
flashing an instant in the late sun—

The dry fly floats and weaves
along the current, till its inevitable end,
and then another cast—

A primal venture: fathers and sons,
removed for a day from civilization,
tapping the root of wilder older ways—

And finally returning along the grassy trail
to the ford, where even the shallows
run treacherous and quick—

All things turn and turn about:

for the crossing in the falling light,
the son lifts the father upon his back.

The God Is a Black Bear

The god is a black bear in the scrub brush
eating blackberries grown fat in summer
catching trout in a rippling rock-strewn creek
cheating the great blue heron of his catch
napping happily in a patch of sun
circled by poplars and thick-plaited pines

The god is a black bear in the old wood
in which I have walked often as a child
in daytime and in dream I saw the god
as he stood and gazed back at me I heard
his deep-belly growl rumble through the trees
We were both surprised that I understood

The god is a black bear on the mountain
which I have climbed in daytime and in dream
through the turnings of every season

I spoke with him again just this morning
He grumbled a secret that I must keep
then he went to sleep in a swatch of sun—

Late Ghost

Nighttime always haunts me slowly to sleep—

Tonight, a late ghost in the moon-writhed oak
mimics a mockingbird, whose own song mimes
a symphony of crickets in the heat
of a midnight swelter in Tennessee.

Fireflies are smothered by a woolen breeze,
enveloping already fevered air.

I sit in small light, try to remember
how the recurring question came to be:

Am I now, this time, the host or the guest
to the late ghost who mocks from moon-coiled tree?

A Quiet in the Weather

    (A night on Terrapin Branch)

There is a quiet in the weather
when the wind draws in its breath,
like the stillness of a watchful cat—

a stillness without tension,
   a waiting
casually
      for the kill.

Do you feel it? It is there
between the beating and the resting
of the pulse, inside
   the shadow's shadow,
behind the owl's luminescent eyes,
    underneath
the glowing moon,
underneath the heavy air,
   muffled in the footfall
      of the prowling lynx.

It is waiting, it is there.

On the far ridge, a coyote howls.
The owl swoops down, talons drawn.
The lynx leaps upon her prey.
The moon
      makes no move at all.

There is a quiet in the weather:
the wind draws in its breath—

The Fawn

The doe brought her wounded fawn for three days
to lie under the twisted hawthorn tree
by the kitchen-corner of our cottage,
while she browsed in the under-brush nearby.

When he followed her in late afternoon
up the narrow ridge-trail to bigger wood,
I could see his right rear leg had been maimed,
flopping as he tried to keep up with her.

The second day, I set out some goat chow
and a pan of water. They came again:
her leading the way warily to where
her child settled, nibbled a bit of grain,

and stayed while she allowed—till the sun strayed
over the western ridgeline, and they left.
On the third morning, the lame fawn was there
by sunup, under the same thorn-apple.

The doe was not to be seen. I kept watch
all day. When the afternoon hour gathered,
the fawn tried to stand and steady himself.
But, during the night, he had been attacked—`

by a coyote, I guessed—and the leg
that had been damaged—was gone. He stumbled,
fell, struggled gamely, gave up—and lay down
in that square of our yard. I shot him quick.

                                              The Fawn ...

And then I sobbed and cried. I laid his body
in the crook of an oak I knew, further
back in the forest. I hoped his mother
might find him there. Years past, I still wonder

why she brought her wounded fawn, three days straight,
to lie under our twisted hawthorn tree.

Dryspell

The noon sky is a cloudless desert.
The sun hammers its stake straight
into the shrunken breastbone of earth.

Pale summer leaves curl like ashes,
    sigh like dust.

The undernourished breeze becomes
a stray dog, panting on its belly
    in yellow grass.

Like fingernails on newspaper,
    parched cicadas rasp.

In a weathered-oak rocker on the porch,
the farmer of far-aging fields
    fitfully naps—

    his fingers a small pile of twigs
    bunched like kindling in his lap,
    a clasped ache of shrinking bones,
    his breath the frail flutter
    of a dying moth—

wishing in his half-awake dreams
he could remember—
remember the old spells
told by his mother:

Dryspell ...

spells for gathering
and thickening the clouds,
for making the rain,

for making the rain
soak into the ground
   like sleep.

Cooler Nights

The nights have grown a snitch cooler,
and the leaves begin to shrink.

Soon they will turn yellow and red,
fall—and float like nimble boats,

riding high on the waterline
to navigate the current,

the clearwater rapids and pools:
a doomed journey—most of them

will never sail past the downstream
property line till drowning.

❧

Deadfall hardwood, cut into rounds
and dragged from the ridge last spring,

has seasoned—ready to be split
and stacked as ricks in the shed.

The chimney has been swept of soot,
though weeks from a laying a fire.

Dry elderberry wine is stored
in racks of dark green bottles.

A winter's worth of garlic braids
have been hung in the stairwell.

❧

Cooler Nights ...

This is a lull between seasons:
not yet fall, though summer's gone—

like holding in a long-drawn breath
before letting go again.

Tonight, a gray-nosed drizzling wind
snuffles a damp handkerchief

around the old cottage, wheezing
like a phlegm-drenched voice between

the cracks in crooked window-frames.
I sit with the cat and a glass

of tawny port to toast this day
I relinquish to the night,

in this breath between the seasons.

Hickory Grain

The clock in hickory grain
tells better time
than metallic gears,
if only we knew how to tell.

Hours meld into days,
seasons fold themselves
into calendars of years
we can pretend to decode.

Our abstractions beguile us
into believing we know
what time is—we don't.
The clock in hickory grain

tells better time: it tells
of sultry summerheat and frost
that kills in winter,
of worms and storms,

ground-swelling rains, floods
that nearly drown the roots—
every weather of its age
before an axe split the bark,

cut its way to the heartwood
and overthrew an elder tree—

so we could count dead-end time
in the memory of hickory grain.

The Rattlesnake

How many months had he made his home
in the raspberry patch we had pruned for years?
How many times might we have passed him,
unaware, in the yard—especially at night?

We knew his tribe lived higher on the ridge,
and we were always watchful
                              when we walked there.
But a prolific band of black kingsnakes
were our close-by neighbors—and they
were deadly enemies of rattlers and copperheads.
We were careful of them in our mowing,
often waiting—setting the mower to idle,
out of gear—while they went their way.

I've sat on the porch steps in the sun
with a kingsnake curled at my feet—unafraid,
having become familiar.
                        From time to time,
I had to mediate a spat between one of them
and our cats.
              We shared a habitat—
also with turkeys, deer, foxes and coyotes,
great blue heron—priest of the creek—
the red-tailed hawk, night-hunter owls,
and a bobcat whose coat was gray and rust.

We learned, over seasons, to live together
along the borders of each other's domiciles.

The Rattlesnake ...

    And so I was surprised by the rattlesnake,
    coiled in rage at the edge of our yard.
    He had been wounded, and pain
    made him mean—so now he struck out
    at whatever came near.
                           I killed him with a hoe.

    I buried his head under a stone,
    and threw his scarred body into the woods
    to be devoured in nature's way.
    And I said a prayer.
                      I always said a prayer
    to whatever spirits might be listening, and care.
    It was not our first tragedy at Terrapin Branch.
    But soon others followed fast—and Death
    came stalking on hard feet, breathing hard,
    until we were wearied by it too much—
    after fifteen years—any longer to stay.

    Times come, and times go, and come again.
    We moved from the country to a far-away town.

    The day we left was a hurried and hollow day,
    battered by a chill spring wind.
                          I called goodbye
    to whatever spirits might care—and I swear
    I heard a scattering of voices call back.

    I think they were sad to see us leave
    on such a hurried and hollow day.

Moving from the Country to the Town

Packing the impracticals
we cannot keep, and the artifacts
that will no longer fit, I confess
that I apologized aloud
to a friendly old cast-iron pot
as I placed it in the box.

∾

Although there is plenty of deadfall on the ridge
to be cut, stacked and seasoned—
today I sold my chainsaws, the axes and the maul.

∾

We invited the neighbors to take
what tools they wanted
from the barn and the shed.

They emptied it all
in less than an hour.

∾

We drove all night in the packed pick-up truck.
When we arrived after sun-up,
there was still leftover snow, tucked
into the shadier corners of the parking lot.

∾

Moving from the Country to the Town ...

    The moving man said: "Where you want us
    to put all this stuff?" Stacks of boxes
    took every square of space on the porch.

    ∽

    The sun sets in a more open sky
    than we have been used to. The stars
    awaken along the northern horizon,
    though dimmed by lights
    of the surrounding town—
    and we imagine the moon
    could peer straight into our windows
    as we sit now at a higher perch.

    In the plush and deepening gloam,
    what can we say to each other but

        "Welcome home."

Elemental Blessing

Power of earth, our lives uphold.
Power of water, wash away blame.
Power of air, with song enfold.
Power of fire, our hearts enflame.

With harm to none, good will to all—
as we wish, may it well befall.

On a Windy Day in a New Place

Layers of weariness lay
like woolen blankets
over my shoulders—a shawl
of heaviness bearing down
on my bones, bearing
me down into deeper ground
where, wrapped in waylaid visions
of lives lived in other lands,
in the swirl of stranger winds
than these, I might rest a while—
I might rest, here, for a while.

Boundary Stones

   (For my father)

I.

The season of your dying was your favorite season,
the weather day of your death bright-eyed: a pheasant
waking from the frost-crisp grass in the sunrise church
of an autumn orchard, who woke to wind-crackling bells
spilling apples from their throats to call down the aisles
of a late corn harvest the hesitant choir of your tears,
the brave homily of your breath—in distant November,
workday morning of the old farm in Pennsylvania.

II.

I wish I remembered less than I do—and could forgive
more than I can. I have been angry with you for so long.
I carry grievances you may not have imagined—
and, if you did, may have wept over them as much as I.

You were too tough, I was too weak—until I learned
to shout my anger back at you, with hard-clenched fists
and a white-knuckled soul, still scarred from that clenching.

Why did you use me to try to justify your life?
Why did I allow it, at such cost to my own?

Father, we were fools.
               In later years we tested
a kind of wary friendship—beer and football afternoons,
hunting in deep mountain snowfall, walking
the briar-lined lanes down on the farm.

Boundary Stones ...

            We would jostle and laugh, and wish
it had always been so.
      It was the best we could do.

And you died too soon.

And in the arms of your dying you did weep
—quietly, not for show—
from sadness, not fear:
knowing you were dying too soon.

III.

The day you died became like a coin
lost in the pocket of a shirt I had misplaced,
or a calendar-page with an appointment erased
but not canceled: an absence discovered
past the due date.   Nothing can be returned.

I think of you less often, and now
more sad than troubled.

But these words I set down
   like boundary stones
to mark a corner of the days you walked.

The season of your dying was your favorite season,
the weather day of your death bright-eyed—

If I Have Found My Way Here

If I have found my way here, I don't know
how—or how to make my way back. No way
back—in all history, there's never been:
the old illusion of Odysseus.

No maps really foretell our pathways,
nor do our recollections recapture
the facts—we are prone to a selective
forgetfulness. Better to let it be.

I am here. The sun still beats in my blood,
and, as I am still able, I beat back.
That and the love of a woman I call
friend—in all history, has there been more?

How I have found my way here, I don't know.
Nor do I know, from here, how I will go—

Bendithia Ni Braid

Lady, your light brightens the lakewater—
reflections of goldenrod cast along
the farther shore, against the green of trees.
There is only a small breeze this morning,
but the geese in their comings and goings
shatter the delicate looking-glass sheen.

I have been troubled, my soul has been torn,
and I ask once again for your blessing,
given long ago in a heavy cloud
of sunfire, wrapping around like a cloak
till I could not stand—but I did not ken
the meaning. I left it, like a realm-coin

from some mysterious land, locked away
in a treasure-box of totems forgot.
Like a petty thief, I come to pick the lock
of memory, to pry open the box
and recover the coin—to remember
all that took place under your sun-mantle

that day, to crack the minted kenning-code.
Now, with a rended soul like torn water,
I sit in a small breeze and watch your face—
mirrored bright in gold and green on the lake,
in clouds and geese and every bright thing—
while turning a coin in my mind, I sing:

Bendithia ni Braid.
Bendithia ni Braid.

Bendithia Ni Braid ...

Bendithia ni: "Bless us ...."

In the Welsh, Brigid became Ffraid—based apparently on a rule for compound words, in this case "Sant-Ffraid." The name may have been first translated into the Welsh (from the Irish Gaelic) as "Braid" (Brai'-eed). Both are Celtic languages. I am not referencing the Christian saint, but the spirit-goddess. In native Welsh, there is also Braint—perhaps derived from Brigantia. I myself feel free to mix languages, and the many names of the Lady—as I understand Her (mostly, I use Breej or Breejah). But I did want to honor the Celtic Welsh, in a small way, as best I can. The reader may substitute as s/he pleases.

Looking Back

Death hides, not
in the future—
but lies in wait,
a shadowy stalker
behind us
in the alleyways,
blind dead-ends
and ringed-in alcoves
of the past—whispering,
always whispering
memories of better times,
while knowing the truth
that time
runs on courses of its own,
betraying equally
both foresight
and remembrance. Death
lies. There is no life
to be found there.

Only you can give to Death,
by the simple turning
of your head,
the respectability
he craves.

Death lies, and lies in wait
always behind us—
like a shadow, drawing us
back. Do not look,
don't turn your head.

Don't you dare look back—

Let Us Let Go

    (For Vivian)

Let us let go
of all that might have been
too diligently ingrained
along the way of our wayward
meandering—all the long days
that have carried us here—
all the times we were sure
we had lost our way—I am sure
now of nothing at all
but you—I am sure of you, not
the person of our past
but just you before me now
in the way that we are—
just the way that we are
and that is enough.

Transmigrations

    (To my ADHD)

Each new moment is a chrysalis
out of which I never know
who, this time in time, I might become—

endless turnings and transmigrations,
quickening sparks of destiny,
making strange fractals of memory

that spin around an empty center:
eye of stillness in the storm,
an in-between of breathlessness before

breaking open, the onslaught renewed,
the tumult I try to keep
a secret for appearances sake—

There in that clear space is the witness
who is no content at all,
whose only gift is to be aware

of the never-ending turbulence,
a subterranean river
of images, ideas and dreams—

each moment a cluttered costume-box,
out of which I never know
what outfit, this time, I might put on.

Be as Air

    Walking the high high wire
        breath after breath

            to placate
    the daily carnival crowd

       just
           let go

of everything of yourself

Be as air

Even if you fall
      without a net

you still may float
deft as a breeze
          all the way down

All Things Are Full of Gods

"All things are full of gods."

—Thales

They sing in the stones and the steel,
whisper in the wires behind the wall,
thread needles with strings of stars,
and hide in the cracks between our thoughts.

They cavort with the potted plants
in the corners of our porch, and dance
like dervishes in the steam
that swirls from a simmering stew.

They laugh in the flash of lightning,
chatter in the rain on window-glass,
lay in the dust on the bookcase
and take long naps with the cats.

In every flip of a coin, or throw
of the dice, Isis-Fortuna has her say.
Chronos ticks in the grandfather clock;
and sure a sprite there is, who chimes the time.

An eager Hermes springs to ecstatic life
whenever the telephone rings.
And what strange visitants watch me now
from behind the computer screen?

(The god who lives in the mirror
might give you a frightening start,
if you catch his flickering glance
in the midst of some vain and foolish act.)

All Things Are Full of Gods ...

There are too many to call all by name
or even to make a guess at their number,
let alone to worship each, one by one—
as if worship were what they wanted.

The world is a vast diaspora
of individualized divinity—
wide-open temple to a ragtag,
footloose and far-flung pantheon.

Every luminous moment is home
to at least one goddess or god—
great or small, guest or host.

All things are full of gods.

And all they wish for from us
is the occasional wink or nod—
at most, a small token for being here,
just for being here—with us.

Now in the Urbs, We Meet New Gods

Now in the Urbs, we meet new gods. The gods
are not new—it is we who are new here,
having lived so long in the countryside.

One might say that we meet old gods anew,
in places we have far been absent from—
and begin to learn, like street signs, their names.

To Greet the Gods

> "Know ye not that ye are gods?
>
> —Hermes Trismegistus

I read a story about a Rastafarian who, when he met someone, greeted them by saying: "Hello, Jah." In one instance, it went something like this—

"Hello, Jah."

"Isn't Jah the Rasta's name for God?"

The Rasta replied: "Yes, Jah."

"But, I'm not God!" the other person exclaimed.

"Is the I sure?" The person didn't know what to say, and the Rasta continued: "Maybe the I is, maybe the I isn't. I 'n' I can't say, and so I prefer to call the I 'Jah', as I choose to see in the I 'Jah'—anyway, just in case."

∽

In a world full of gods—

many whose names we do not know,
whose appearances, like sparks, come and go
now as one, now as another,
too quick for our eyes, unskilled and slow,
to keep up with the flame-and-shadow show—

the most proper greeting and invocation
might just be:
           "Hello. How are you?
            And how have we come here?"

New Pagan Gods Are Dancing

New pagan gods are dancing
round the rag-fires of my dreams.
They have not whispered their names,
but I catch their eyes, glancing
from behind the glamoured flames—
and, to my sleep-sight, it somehow seems
they know whom I've now become,
and how far I am from home.

The new gods are not unkind—
will not uproar gentle sleep,
call you out to wakefulness,
or cause glad dreams to unwind—
won't disturb at all unless
there is some promise you need to keep,
or some dark danger has come
to bind you from finding home.

New friends, but from older times,
whose names are only unknown
because forgotten, they smile
to hear me make these rhymes,
wondering for all this while
if I might remember on my own
whence both they and I have come,
and how to find our way home.

Spirits and Sprites

Turn your head quickly—
look with just your left eye,
but neither peer nor stare.

If you don't see us,
try it again.

If you don't see us,
we are still here—

Bast

    Stone cat on the mantle
    brooding, blessing
    blessing the room
    like an Egyptian goddess—

    in another universe
    another consciousness

    She is alive.

Strange Poems

Two cats, sharing my desk with me,
typing with feet and tails on the keyboard:

what strange poems
                in stranger tongues
        scroll across the screen!

Tuatha Dé Danann

> "The truth is not known, beneath the sky of stars, whether they were of heaven or earth."
>
> —*The Book of Invasions* (circa 1150 CE)

We are the fallen angels.
We are the tribe of Danu—
bringer of sun-fire, earth-fire,
water-fire and fire in the blood—
who wakens the dawn of life.

We have forgotten our names.

Once we dwelt in the green mists
among apples and the oak,
and in the chattering streams,
the stones that sang so softly,
the breeze that lifted the hawk,
the flame that burnt in the veins of grass.

Before that, we dwelt among the stars.

Now we live in the cities,
gliding between the lights—
you might catch a glimpse of us
if your eyes are quick enough.
We can be found often in the parks
where the earthen fire still burns
in the roots and veins of grass,
and behind the bark of trees.

Tuatha Dé Danann ...

But also we conceal ourselves
in concrete cocoons, shining steel
and glass, peering through the smoke
of darkened windows at a world
turned marketplace of all desires,
where hardly could we be known.

Sometimes we might almost look like you—
except for the lightning that flashes,
like fireworks down a deep well,
in the deep well of our eyes.

We are lucky to find each other
in this world, and many walk alone.

Our greeting is a secret song,
sung underneath the threshold
of your ears—or we just nod and pass,
passing by some ancient kin whose name,
locked long ago in a cratering star,
we no longer know how to set free.

We are the fallen angels.
We are the tribe of Danu,
goddess of the fire of life.
We have forgotten our names.

We dwell unknown among you.
If you meet us, you are blest.

Janus

> *Omnia quae videmus et imaginamus modo imagines reflectuntur per infinitatem speculorum sunt.*

I.

Janus is an old Roman god who rules
over doorways, windows, all beginnings—
who opens portals, made of light, we traverse

through fulgent mirrors imaging our worlds,
both far away and near—and in between,
where, as figments, we abide: in the in-between.

In every mirror, many mansions shine
with many passageways from room to room—
an endless, gleaming all-in-all in which we dream.

(When you realize how the net is twined
—mirrored corridors braiding round and round—
none of your dreams or memories will seem the same.)

II.

Janus peers both ways through the looking-glass
of a brightly-polished sun to descry
the goings-on in all the secret nooks-of-dark

and well-lit avenues of fate—although
he may not speak of them: you have to gaze
into his luminous, mirroring eyes—

                                          Janus ...

where you might see what's gone before, as well
as what could come—doors be open or be shut—
as we cross the thinly-glossed thresholds of our time,

because time itself has countless facets,
clocks with unnumbered faces, spinning round
as we wait—for divine
                    Janus to turn his head.

A Hole in the World

> "Every angel is terrifying."
>
> —Rainer Maria Rilke, *Duino Elegies*

There was a hole
in the world and I
looked in—

and the eye looking back,
blindingly ablaze

like the eye of a star
from a far zodiac,
zooming dangerously near
to gaze
through a hole in the world,

was my own—

instantly afire
with angelic light.

Staring Hard at the Chessboard

    (For Richard Parker)

Staring hard at the chessboard
suddenly become
                surreal:
  a painting by Dali
with too many dimensions,
        as time
              ticks
                        far away
    into space—

The squares are melting, misshapen;
the black Knight is missing his head;
a cactus rears up where a Bishop stood;
my King turns into a hairy dwarf,
hiding inside a gingerbread Rook;
my Queen, donning a coat of thick fur,
    shapeshifts
           into the goddess Artio,
roaming restlessly a dark briar-wood;
and all the Pawns
                are toadstools
      wearing red hats,
                    playing cards
        while puffing on meerschaum pipes—

Staring hard at the chessboard, desperate
to recover from the last blunder—
losing my Jester to a fork—it all
goes quickly clear when I remember

Staring Hard ...

    what you told me once: that I'm always
       more dangerous
            when down a piece.

The clock clicks back to its place, the board
squares up, the pieces reclaim their shapes,
my reverie ends—and, with a boldness born
  of walkabout in dreamtime,

    I make my next move.

Whimsy

'Twas one of the Whimsies flew into town,
dazzling the people with her sapphire gown—

"Ah, those Whimsy girls," the good town-folk said,
"so alive with laughter, though they're all dead!"

"Sure, I am only a ghost of myself,
but I shan't sit still like salt on the shelf!"

So said Miss Whimsy, twirling upside down,
dazzling as a dream in her sapphire gown.

Two Minds

Always hopelessly of at least two minds—

unable to decide
among those strident claims to truth
by partisans so immunized
from chafing doubt they need not look
a hazardous question straight in the eye—

unable even to insist
that my own ideas will last the day
before their mist-etched letters fall—
to float up again in shape-shifted form:
flimsy idols that for a time
entice as true as those that went before—

I seem always hopelessly of two minds—
or more—and I cannot decide
if that is a virtue or flaw.

At least I can never buckle belief
onto anyone as ironclad law—

Beware the Single-Faced Person

Always beware the single-faced person—

as you might beware the lurking threat
of false shallows, concealing a breakneck
plunge neath a sprightly web of moon-spun lace:
a shimmer thinly flittering across
the frail skin of a quickly flowing stream.

The world we romp is seldom as it seems.
Nor are we: we all wear many faces
to others—and to ourselves just as well.
It is both ancient and civilized dress.
Duplicity only becomes deceit
under the pretense of straightforwardness.

Be wary of those who show just one face,
as you would shallows in a moonlit race.

Far from those Celtic Shores

Far from those Celtic shores, the Sun,
with an armful of spears,
peers into the dark horizon.

What crouching hordes are gathered there
along the battlements
of anvil-black clouds, awaiting

the deep-throated blast of the horn
to signal the attack?
What archers have drawn their long bows

to loose their lightning-tipped arrows
against the warriors
forming along the sea of light?

Once again a war unwanted.
Once again the old fear.
Once again the armies arrayed.

Far from those Celtic shores, the Sun,
shining eyes full of tears,
peers into the dark horizon.

Go Down Dying

Next time, she'll go down dying—

warrior pain-honed,
    body a forge-fired spear
wielded to every quarter
    with fierce piercing cries—

Next time, she'll stalk her attackers—
    leopard circling back
to track the baying pack
    until she catches them,

hurling herself
    to every quarter
with fierce piercing cries—

Not again will she submit,
    permit to be captured,
used—refusing surrender
    to either flattery or fright,

next time, she'll do battle—
    no Valkyrie serving the slain
in Valhalla, but spear-fighter
    giving no quarter

as she abandons herself
    with fierce piercing cries
to the fury of the fray—

Next time, she'll go down dying.

Singing of Sun and Fire

    Yes, I sing often
        of sun and fire,
           drum and flame—
    and redundancies abound,
    as also in my daily round.

    These are my themes,
    these are my dreams:
        spirit of sunfire
           in the drum and the flame.

Tabula Rasa

They have cleared the brush down to the lake,
and taken all but a few mature trees.
I am told they are going to build houses.

But for now, in early, sun-misted summer,
it is a rough-cut meadow of green
sloping down to the green ruffled water,

and the hawk who roosts in the forest
on the other shore hunts freely,
for a time, over the open grass.

Now is no more than a changeable scene.
And all that we can see or know
is just an erasable tableau.

Mae

(For Jennifer)

When you were a young woman you stole a name.

You were never to be forgiven—
not by the proper people who lived on the hill,
nor by the son whose love you lost
(though he at times told your stories with grudging pride—
but also a grimace, as if he'd stubbed his toe).
But you would never allow them to make you bow.

Later you smuggled some green stones
from out of a southern country, to wear
on your rings when you went to town.
You bet on the sulkies and horses,
and played a crafty hand of poker—
and you never lost the farm, with the house
of tinted windows and whole-oak beams,
and the graves of our ancestors,
some of whose names were worn away smooth
into weathered white stone
by more than two centuries of calloused
and wind-pummeled northeastern seasons.

You practiced a country witchcraft
imported from Europe, and ladled
with local roots and strange signs.
You were a gourmet cook who delighted
in large meals and other grand gestures,
meant to prick the Protestant disapproval.
There was always bourbon in the sideboard,
bitters, vermouth and various liqueurs.

Mae ...

You lived as large as you could the old truth:
"Living well is the best revenge."

(When I was still in school, you suggested
that I hire on as your chauffeur
for a long trip out west to the casinos.
But I was too proper then, and stayed in school.)

You outlived your son—and almost the century—
unforgiven, outspoken and unbent.
Your secrets would have died with you—
that was how the family had it planned—
but you leaked them to an accomplice
for temporary safekeeping
until the boxes could be unpacked.
So now I have your secrets as keepsakes,
and some of your recipes as well.

Once, on a visit too near to your leaving,
I remember getting lost in your gaze—
as if I were peering unprepared
into a faraway mystical place.
You asked me, "What are you looking at in there?"
I had no words. My mind was held still.
Then you laughed and said,
"Well, you're just like I am, you know."

(Sometimes inside my soul I hear
a voice that sounds like my own,
whispering, as in a waking dream,
"I wish it were so,
I wish it were so—")

Mae ...

> They tried to lock up your lawless love
> like Eleanor of Aquitaine,
> in a tower of well-chiseled lies.
> You were to be visited rarely:
> on a weekend or a holiday,
> for appearances' sake—
> the appropriate pretenses
> to be observed at all times.
>
> But you kept breaking the locks.
>
> You had a big car, and even after eighty
> you could drive as fast as your age.
> One summer you drove a small boy many miles
> to a carnival-park, where you allowed him
> the afternoon's hours to ride all the rides.
> It was dark when we got back to the farm—
> and I slept the whole way back.

∾

> I imagine you now, the seat pulled up close,
> hurling that car through the stars,
> as young as you were when you stole a name—
> travelling west, always west—and laughing
> to know that I at least
> learned of your secrets, and your love.

Mae ...

(And maybe one day down that road,
while there still are westward stars to aim for,
you will again want a chauffeur—)

———————

"Living well ...," George Herbert (1593 – 1633)

Then There Is the Waiting

Then there is the waiting,
like staring down a long stairwell
into a squeezed distance,
wondering if the time will come
on soft shoes quietly up the steps:
a long-awaited question
weighted down by doubt,
the heavy ticking of an age-worn clock
that has not chimed for years—

Meanwhile the swallows
are noisily building their nest
under the eaves outside my window,
hidden from the intruding sky,
unmindful of my brooding—
or the years of hours now
creeping up the stairs to ask me
what I have been waiting for.

Brigid in the City

I saw you strolling among the street-front stores,
window shopping in your sun-wrapped shawl.

The air shone briefly brighter, shimmering
where you walked—that's how I knew it was you.

Isles of the Blest

> The Sun shuffles through the alleys and streets—
> transient traveler in a fading frock,
> wandering once again into the West
> where, it is told, all visitors are blest,
> and even a poor man's purse of dull coin
> can purchase a new spirit, burnished bright—
> but only for those brave fools who'd follow
> a homeless stranger through alleys and streets,
>
> beyond the town, past boundaries invoked
> by those kings and priests who fear and condemn
> the grace of a sinless, borderless place
> beyond the bars of their sanctified space—
>
> Now I have followed the Sun far into the West,
> where I wayfare still—among the Isles of the Blest.

Unpacking for the Journey

How many things must I leave behind
to travel
      light enough
            like dust
to cover the distance?

How far across the desert
  as the crow flies?

I hear of other travelers
who have made the trek,
and of those
    who never dared.
Nobody tells of the ones
who died along the way,
      or where their bones
lie buried in the sand.

I test the weight of my life:
it still hangs heavy
      on my back.
  What else
      must I take out?

A better question? What
can I leave in?

Unpacking for the Journey ...

> "Only as you go will you find
> what you can carry:
>
> > water
> > air
> > light
> > a few prayers, visions.
>
> "A companion
> can help to carry more:
>
> > love
> > words
> > healing
> > hope
> >
> > someone to sing with
> > when the stars
> > lie buried in the night."

The Word-Bag

> (For Laurie Clements)

Just about the time I'm ready
to pack up the old word-bag
and shove it back out of sight
on a dusty shelf—with worn-out shoes
and shopping lists, board games
with missing pieces, suits of clothes
that have not fit for years,
and other memories best left
stacked in a keyless, locked closet
or folded away at the bottom
of some forgotten drawer
in the abandoned furniture
of one of my many past lives—

you go and write another poem
that, like knuckles rapping on the wall,
finds a hollow space where some lost breath
has too long been held, hidden
in a secret passage I thought
I had sealed off—but that harbors
a ghost who will not rest
until the proper words are wrought,
even in my own uneasy voice.

And so, I take up the old word-bag—
slinging a strap over my shoulder,
feeling the weary weight settle,
and my bones settle—and sigh.
I don't know what else to do
but to set out again

The Word-Bag ...

    through the understory of my mind,
    searching for fresh syllables, runes
    widely scattered like acorns
    in a dark and trackless oak-wood,
    to stuff into my well-worn bag—

    for the backward witchcraft curse
    attached to this sack I have kept
    is this: it is heavier empty—
    and only new words lighten the load.

A Man with Seven Sticks

(Based on a Tarot card)

A man with seven sticks must hold his dreams
somehow aloft amid the fidgeting thoughts
assailing his mind: skittering winter winds
that flutter the window curtains, slipping
inside to chill the edges of the room.

Unseen forces are arrayed against him
from without and within. His own clumsy
doubts confuse the path he must trek—the way
that a thick swirling snowfall befuddles
the sight, as he struggles through a thicket

of briarthorn in the darkening wood.
Did he dare make a stand, blind, where he stood?

Or must he keep going through the long night,
fighting the brambles till wakening light?

Cage of Swords

      (Based on a Tarot card)

Hemmed in and hoodwinked,
hands bound by braided cords, caged
in a ring of blindly gleaming blades
she can sense but cannot see—

if only her eyes could be unmasked,
she might slice her bonds
on the very scimitars
betrayers planted to impale her—

and set herself free.

Magister Fortunae

> (For Nick)

The Master of Luck: his card has been laid,
the dice have been thrown, the wheel has been spun.
Before he'll dare see the numbers thus made,
the moment has come to place his next bet.

He has enough chips—already bought in,
as he has been from the hour it began,
till the final coup that will end the bout.
We all play in the game, willing or not,

the contours of our stake chosen by fate—
but we have a chance to win against chance,
no matter how slim it seems—the secret
is contrarian: bet against the house.

The Master of Luck: his fate has been laid,
now he's the gambler—to play or be played.

Coda:

No one is really the master of Luck,
but the Lady loves those who play with pluck.

Butterfly Effects

We've come a long long way on whirling winds
churned by a million million butterflies,
bearing us as we are to this moment—

> no grand predictable patterns; no maps
> drawn along dialectical ley lines;
> no divine destiny laid down by gods
> or fate; no pristine genealogies
> that travel unmixed with story and myth
> from our beginning such a far way back—
> We make all the maps, and pretend
> the world has been measured by our making.

A million million butterflies
have brought us here, and will carry us on—
with or without our efforts to band them,
to bend them to the contours of our will,
or to banish them from our convictions.

Stretch out your arms: that is the only world
you can know—really: just in that space,
just in that time. And then the butterfly
will stir herself into flight—and the gales
that arise from myriads of breezes
will change, before tomorrow, what we thought
must be both irrevocable and true,

scattering into unforeseen fractals
our most deeply cherished cartographies.

Butterfly Effects ...

And beyond that space of your outstretched arms
simply say: "I do not know." That is all.
A shimmering, radiant clarity
—enlightenment of the awen light—
may then begin to illumine your soul.

> Within that single magickal circle
> of your open, momentary embrace,
> just dance and love and heal as best you can.

A million million butterflies
have already whirled away all the rest—

Coda:

We, too, of course, are only butterflies
who've come a long way on many breezes,
and the breezes that carry us from here
will have in them just the barest zephyr—
soon to be untraceable—from our wings.

111

Wherever All the Rivers Run

Wherever all the rivers run—or how
they find their way, or whence they may have sprung—

there is an ocean to which they will come
in time, if even only for a time

before they trace their long pathways again—
or new ones. Somewhere is a burning sea

from which star-seeded sparks of life are flung,
and as well return—until it may be

they will journey once more, to separate
and mate, and mingle into many streams.

Oceans of water or conflagration:
uncountable droplets or shattered stars—

*How tragic for the single flame to fear
annihilation in the larger fire,*

*or waterdrop to be afraid to fall
again into the vastness of the sea.*

Belief

(An etymological poem)

What is belief except to give leave
to what your own heart's desire
would lief allow for you to follow,
and to hallow always with your love?

That is as much as I will believe—
so long as beauty is safely left,
her colorful tapestries, without
furlough, to weave. As for all the rest:

An it will harm none, do as ye lief
and may all be well—beyond belief.

As the Moon Waxes

As the moon waxes now toward fullness,
turning on its primordial axis
in ever-retracing, returning rounds,
I remember the child I left behind—

the child who peered outward with frightened eyes
as first the world, and then I, betrayed him—
his eagerness crushed like a broken toy,
the wonder of playfulness discarded

to fit the demands of more serious
endeavors—and years lost to siren songs
of what must be and what must not—failing
at once both freedom and obligation.

Now as the moon waxes toward the wild,
a world-weary man limps home to the child.

Epilogue – Becoming the Sun

Now my own spirit
    has waxed and waned
and may wax untamed
    again in season

as I keep singing
    of the wild and the sun

    Becoming the hawk
    who becomes the sun

    hawk made of flame
    spirit and drum

    swift currents of light
    wind-fire in my veins

    sharp-singing cry
    kindling my spine

    caught in my eyes
    a far-seeing dream

    deep in my marrow
    drumbeat of the sun

I am still singing
I am still singing
    of the wild and the sun.

Acknowledgments

Although the author has lifetimes of acknowledgments that should be made, these will have to do for now, as pertain to this book—

Mary Nilsen, of Zion Publishing—without whose professionalism, patience and grace, these words you would not be reading.

My brother, Jeff, and Laurie Clements—who have both encouraged me to keep writing over the years, and who have shared their own works with me to gently prod me on.

AllPoetry.com—where earlier versions of a few of these poems were presented and critiqued: thanks to that forum, and all fellow-poets who offered their comments.

Richard Parker—my old, dear friend and chess-nemesis who said: "I really like reading your poems." (That was a needed boost, my friend!)

Vivian—spouse, best friend and "First Editor," who has not only encouraged me, but saved a bunch of early poems that would otherwise have been lost, and was the first one to read through the whole manuscript of this book and offer precious criticism and insight. She also lived with me through many of the experiences described (albeit in metaphor) herein, especially our life together on Terrapin Branch. All my love, My Love!

All the Spirits—too many to name, and many whose names are not known, but who have made themselves known in grace—as I feel you surrounding me now, is it too paltry to just say: "Thank you"? Because I have no other words, in this place and momentary time. Nevertheless, I believe you know . . .

www.ingramcontent.com/pod-product-compliance
Lightning Source LLC
Chambersburg PA
CBHW071707040426
42446CB00011B/1953